L I F E W A Y S

The Iroquois

R A Y M O N D   B I A L

BENCHMARK BOOKS

MARSHALL CAVENDISH
NEW YORK

SERIES CONSULTANT: JOHN BIERHORST

ACKNOWLEDGMENTS

This book would not have been possible without the generous help of a number of individuals and organizations that have dedicated themselves to preserving the culture of the Iroquois. I would like to especially thank Karen Mattila and Rose Nicholas of the Ska-Nah-Doht Iroquoian Village in Ontario, Canada, for their generous help with this book, including permission to make photographs at this wonderful site and to adapt the two stories used in this book. I am also indebted to the staff at Sainte Marie Among the Iroquois for sharing key resources with me. I would also like to acknowledge the assistance of the National Archives, the Library of Congress, and the Philbrook Museum for providing a number of illustrations.

I am very much indebted to my editor Kate Nunn for her enthusiasm and encouragement of this series. As always, I would like to thank my wife, Linda, and my children Anna, Sarah, and Luke for their shining presence in my life.

Cover photos: Raymond Bial

The photographs in this book are used by permission and through the courtesy of: Office of Museums and Historic Sites/Onondaga County Parks Department, Liverpool, New York: 1, 90-91, 100-101, 103. Ska-Nah-Doht Iroquoian Village, Ontario, Canada: 6, 30(bottom), 49, 50, 57, 66(top), 70, 88-89. Raymond Bial: 8-9, 14-15, 17, 19, 20, 22-23, 24, 27, 28, 29, 30(top), 30-31, 53, 54-55, 58, 59, 60, 61, 66(bottom), 69, 73, 76, 78-79, 81, 86, 108-109; The Philbrook Museum of Art, Tulsa, Oklahoma: 11, 46. Art Resource/National Museum of American Art: 33, 36, 40. Corbis-Bettmann: 39. Corbis-Bettmann/UPI: 117. The Woodland Cultural Centre, Brantford, Ontario: 42, 44-45, 64, 106-107. New York State Museum: 43. Library of Congress: 93, 94, 113, 116. Colorado Historical Society: 112. Iroquois Indian Museum: 115.

This book is respectfully dedicated
to all the people who have worked
to keep alive the traditional lifeways
and helped others to understand
the spirit of the Iroquois people.

Contents

Author's Note

At the dawn of the twentieth century, Native Americans were thought to be a vanishing race. However, despite four hundred years of warfare, deprivation, and disease, American Indians have not gone away. Countless thousands have lost their lives, but over the course of this century the populations of native tribes have grown tremendously. Even as American Indians struggle to adapt to modern Western life, they have also kept the flame of their traditions alive—the language, religion, stories, and the everyday ways of life. An exhilarating renaissance in Native American culture is now sweeping the nation from coast to coast.

The Lifeways books depict the social and cultural life of the major nations, from the early history of native peoples in North America to their present-day struggles for survival and dignity. Historical and contemporary photographs of traditional subjects, as well as period illustrations, are blended throughout each book so that readers may gain a sense of family life in a tipi, a hogan, or a longhouse.

No single book can comprehensively portray the intricate and varied lifeways of an entire tribe, or nation. I only hope that young people will come away with a deeper appreciation for the rich tapestry of Indian culture—both then and now—and a keen desire to learn more about these first Americans.

1. Origins

A blend of lakes, rivers, and forests, the home country of the Iroquois was known for its striking beauty.

"Turtle Island"

LONG AGO, BEFORE THE EARTH CAME TO BE, A HUSBAND AND WIFE, who were expecting a child, lived in the Sky World. In the center of the Sky World stood a great tree with four white roots stretching north, south, east, and west, in the directions of the wind. It was a sacred tree, not to be touched by anyone, from which grew many kinds of leaves, fruits, and flowers. One day, the woman was gathering seeds and berries but also desired some bark from the root of the tree. She persuaded her husband to scrape the bark for her, but as he dug at the root, the floor of the Sky World collapsed. Gazing into the opening, the husband and wife were astonished that, far below, there was only water and the creatures who could live in or on it. Bending down for a closer look, the woman lost her balance and fell through the hole in the sky. She was caught by a flock of swans, which, flying wing tip to wing tip, made a feathery raft and carried her aloft.

But there was no land, only water below in which swam the fish and animals. The woman could neither fly nor swim, and the birds didn't know what to do with her. Finally, a turtle swam up and said, "There is room on my back." So the swans gently placed her on its shell. Realizing that there must be earth on which the woman could live, the creatures of the world below plunged deep into the water searching for soil. Again and again they dove, but only the muskrat, its lungs nearly bursting, was able to reach bottom and bring up a little mud in its paws.

"Place the earth on my back," the turtle said. The muskrat did

Creation Legend, *painted by Tom Two-Arrows (Onondaga) in 1946. At the heart of Iroquois culture, the creation story recounts how North America was formed on the back of a turtle.*

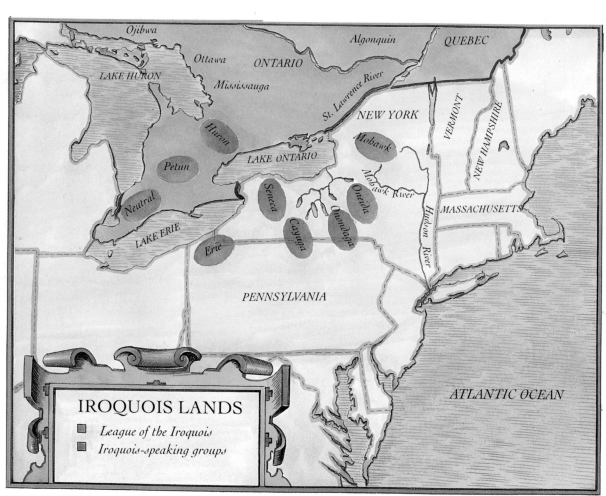

IROQUOIS LANDS

■ League of the Iroquois
■ Iroquois-speaking groups

The traditional homelands of each of the five original members of the League of the Iroquois extended over much of what is now New York.

so, and the woman began to walk in a circle, in the same direction as the sun. The mud grew and grew until it became Turtle Island, which is the Iroquois name for their home in North America. The woman dropped the seeds and berries she had carried from the Sky World, and they sprouted into the plants and trees that now cover the earth. The children of the woman later became the *Hodenosaunee* (pronounced hoe-de-no-SHOW-nee), which means "people of the longhouse." This is what the Iroquois call themselves, and how the land and people came to be.

OVER A THOUSAND YEARS AGO, THE TRIBES OF THE IROQUOIS MOVED into the thick green forests of what is now central New York. Thousands of years earlier, people from Asia had crossed a land bridge that joined Asia and Alaska, or had sailed by boat to the Alaskan coast. Their descendants spread south and eastward over the continent of North America, eventually forming numerous Native American groups, including the Iroquois. The Iroquois (pronounced EAR-ah-koy in the United States and EAR-ah-kwah in Canada) drove out the Native Americans who then occupied the region of streams and lakes between the Adirondack Mountains and Niagara Falls that is now in upstate New York. Many North American tribes spoke Iroquoian languages, but only five northeastern tribes became part of the powerful League of the Iroquois. The five tribes, or nations, and their location, east to west, were the Mohawk, Oneida, Onondaga, Cayuga (pronounced kigh-YOU-gah), and Seneca. The center of the League was in

Onondaga country near present-day Syracuse. The Onondaga were the "fire-keeping" nation of the Iroquois. Around 1722 the Tuscarora joined the League as a sixth member after they were driven by settlers from present-day Virginia and North Carolina. These tribes gradually expanded their territory around the lower Great Lakes of Huron, Ontario, and Erie, as well as Lake Champlain and Lake George. They also settled along the St. Lawrence River, primarily in what are now the provinces of Ontario and Quebec in Canada. Some branches of the League eventually

Groves of birch trees with white trunks extending skyward brightened the landscape around Iroquois villages, which were carved out of the deep hardwood forests.

extended as far west as Wisconsin and as far south as the Allegheny Mountains in Pennsylvania. At its height in 1680 there were between 10,000 and 17,000 individual members in the League of the Iroquois.

The Iroquois vigorously defended their lands from surrounding tribes. To the north in Canada lived the Hurons, who became rival traders and bitter enemies of the Iroquois, as well as allies of the French. West of the Iroquois were the Tobacco Indians and the Neutrals, so-called because they tried to stay out of the wars

between the Iroquois and the Hurons. The Susquehanna, or Conestoga, lived in what is now central Pennsylvania, along with the Erie Indians.

The name *Iroquois* is a French version of *Irinakhoiw*, meaning "poisonous snakes." The name was given to them by their bitter enemies, the Ojibwa. Although there were many differences among the tribes of the league, the Iroquois spoke basically the same language and shared a similar way of hunting, gathering, farming, and waging war. They made their homes in the sprawling forests of elm, hickory, maple, and birch trees, beneath the ragged branches of hemlocks and white pines. The forests provided food, shelter, and clothing, as well as tools, weapons, and medicine. Strong and agile, the Iroquois were somewhat taller than other North American Indians as well as Europeans at the time of their first encounter. They had no written language, other than the wampum belts on which they recorded their history, so they relied on their excellent memories. They were able to vividly recall stories and long speeches, word for word, many years after hearing them.

The Iroquois valued courage, strength, endurance, and independence. They could be very cruel to their enemies, yet gentle, considerate, and highly cooperative among their own people. In large villages of a thousand or more people, they worked together constructing longhouses and providing for each other. Like other native peoples of North America, they felt a spiritual kinship with the natural world. Although they hunted animals and gathered plants, they did not try to dominate their environment but found a place for themselves among all living things.

The People and the Land

For a thousand years the Iroquois people lived in the forests around the southern Great Lakes and the valley of the St. Lawrence River. The hardwoods of the eastern forest—maple, elm, ash, hickory, chestnut, and beech—blended with stands of birch trees and the eternal green of hemlock, pine, and spruce forests to the north. The elm tree, which provided bark for longhouses and canoes, had special religious meaning: at the center of the earth stood the Great Elm, with its huge, arching branches.

The Iroquois were at home in the green forests that blanketed most of eastern North America in the 1600s. The trees provided wood for longhouses and fuel for fires, as well as handles for tools and weapons.

There were no high mountains, only gentle hills, from which to spot an enemy or welcome a friend. There were also many rivers and streams, forming a vast water network among the lakes. The Iroquois could easily paddle canoes throughout their territory to trade corn, beans, or animal pelts with their friends and make war on their enemies. Although trees had to be cleared to build villages near the rivers, the land was fertile and easily worked with their stone tools. The Iroquois relied on crops of corn, beans, and squash, but they also hunted and gathered in the woods and fields.

The people of the longhouse lived within nature. The cycle of their lives revolved around four clearly defined seasons. In the spring, the sap flowed and, like delicate green lace, the buds emerged on the trees. The earth softened, warmed, and was made ready to receive seeds. In early summer, cherries and June berries, including wild strawberries and raspberries, were gathered before the long stretches of hot, dry weather. As July temperatures soared, ears of corn quickly ripened on the stalk.

In the autumn, the trees became a panorama of brilliant red, yellow, and orange foliage. Corn leaves and stalks faded to tan, pumpkins glowed orange on the damp ground, and drying beans rattled in their shells. Women harvested their fields and gathered crab apples, along with the last of the blackberries, before the first chill winds from the west swept over them. In winter, the jagged pines were silhouetted against the purple sky, and the snows fell steadily, filling the valleys and spreading a soft white blanket over

During autumn, when the leaves of the sumac bushes became as brilliantly red as flames, women harvested corn, beans, and squash. They also gathered the last of the fruits and berries that grew wild at the edge of the forest.

the land. Frozen rivers and lakes disappeared under the drifts, and people settled around their longhouse fires, trudging only short distances in their snowshoes.

Whatever the time of year, the Iroquois imbued their world with spiritual meaning. Above in the Sky World lived the

Men made clearings near the village. Girls and women then worked the fertile soil with flint-blade hoes, forming small hills in which they planted crops against a backdrop of forest trees.

right-handed twin, who was the Master of Life (also known as He Who Holds Up the Sky and Great Creator). In the Sky World, too, were Our Grandmother the Moon and Our Elder Brother the Sun. The land itself rested on the back of the turtle. The corn spirits watched over the villages and fields, and the little people and masked spirits dwelled in the forest. Below the land lived Flint, the evil, left-handed twin of the Master of Life—devious and stubborn, his body covered with sores.

The forest was the domain of men—hunters and warriors—who trotted along paths beneath the canopy of branches. Only faint shafts of light filtered through the leaves of the towering trees, whose trunks stood like columns holding up a high green ceiling. There was little brush on the forest floor—just a cushion of leaves or pine needles springy underfoot. It was a dim world, cool and nearly silent.

The clan mothers ruled the clearings where the villages and fields were found. Here, the earth absorbed the heat of the sun glinting brightly in the clear blue sky. The open places rang with the laughter of children and the talk of women working around the longhouses. The forest reached into the unknown, while the clearing was familiar and secure—it was home.

Whether forest or clearing, all the earth was like the air, necessary for survival but belonging to no one. The Iroquois never imagined that land could be bought and sold.

2. Villages

Within the villages each longhouse sheltered several families.

IN EARLY TIMES, VILLAGES WERE LITTLE MORE THAN HAMLETS OF FIFTY or so people. Later, between about 1550 and 1675, several hundred people might live in a village or as many as three thousand. The villages often lay on high ground for protection from attack, near streams where fresh drinking water could be found. As farmers, the Iroquois did not have to move continually like the hunting people of the plains. However, the village had to be moved every ten to fifteen years, when the soil of the fields became exhausted and game was scarce. High log fences called palisades surrounded each village. With sharp points extending skyward, the logs were set into the ground and lashed together to create a fortress. Along the inside of the walls were high platforms where lookouts could warn villagers of enemy attack. Sometimes, the Iroquois designed entrances as a maze to confuse enemies and slow their progress into the village. Within the palisades, they constructed a number of large dwellings called longhouses, as well as storage buildings and sweat lodges. They set up racks for drying and stretching animal hides and dug pits for burying garbage. Villages were often quite large; many had 30 to 150 longhouses.

There were ten clans among the people of the longhouse: Turtle, Bear, Wolf, Beaver, Deer, Hawk, Ball, Heron, Snipe, and Eel. Not all clans were represented in every nation—only the Turtle, Bear, and Wolf were found in all five nations of the original League

The Iroquois had to be vigilant in protecting their villages from attack. Sentries climbed log steps to lookout posts inside the palisades, where they watched for approaching war parties.

of the Iroquois. All the people in a clan considered themselves related, even if they were originally from a different nation, and they remained members of their clan, or "longhouse family," for life. Children of all families in the clan grew up as brothers and sisters, and a large clan might occupy several longhouses in the village. The men in the clan hunted together in the forest while the women and children worked as a group in the garden.

Villages were lively places, filled with the bustling sounds of work—the thud of mortar and pestle as women ground corn, the scrape of flint blades on deer hides, and the chop of a stone ax. There was the crackle of the fires, and the air was tinged with the smell of wood smoke. Clanspeople enjoyed living and working together. Within the longhouses, they gladly shared food and fire.

Longhouses

About 80 to 150 feet long and 20 to 30 feet wide, longhouses had curved roofs and low entrances at each end either fitted with bark doors and wooden hinges or hung with the skins of deer or bear. A carving of the animal representing the clan living in the longhouse was mounted above the doorway so that visitors from other villages could find shelter among their own people. Usually built in late spring or early summer, longhouses were made of wooden poles covered with shingles of elm bark. Saplings lashed to the frame held down the bark. To waterproof the longhouse, cracks in the bark were sealed with sticky sap from spruce trees. There was a row of smoke holes in the curved roof, each of which

During the summer, the longhouse deflected the intense sunlight; during the winter, the windowless building provided a warm refuge from the wind and snow.

was covered with a piece of bark that could be nudged aside with a pole from inside the longhouse.

Fifteen to twenty families lived in each longhouse. A center aisle ran the length of the impressive building, separating the families on either side and providing a place for eight to ten fire pits used for cooking and heat. After 1700, the Iroquois built smaller longhouses with three to four fire pits, housing fewer families because of population loss from disease and war. Council

When erecting a new longhouse, a group of men first built a sturdy, interconnected framework by bending and lashing wood poles together.

meetings were also held in these central spaces, or in special longhouses reserved for ceremonies.

Set about four feet off the ground, platforms for sleeping and storing personal belongings were built along the inside walls of the longhouse. Sheets of elm bark were used to divide the space into compartments. Overhead, a bright tapestry of red, yellow, and purple braided corn, dried squash, and smoked meat hung from the rafters and crossbeams, along with items such as snowshoes and cradleboards. The typical Iroquois longhouse also held clay pots for cooking and carrying water, wooden bowls for serving

Sheets of elm bark were stripped from trees, cut into rough shingles, and laid over the frame of the longhouse. The shingles were then securely tied down with saplings.

food, burden straps for cradleboards, sharpened bone tools, and perhaps a deer jaw used to scrape dried corn kernels from cobs or a birchbark storage chest acquired by trade with the Algonquins. Pots, kettles, baskets, clothes, weapons, and other possessions were kept on the platform. Squash and other foods might also be stored on the ground under the platform or in bins made of hollow logs.

People slept on cornhusk mats, covering themselves in the winter with bearskins to keep themselves warm against the wind blowing through the cracks between the elm bark shingles.

A row of fire pits lined the earthen center aisle of the longhouse, and corn was hung overhead to dry in the heat (top left). Food and belongings were stored along the interior walls (bottom left). People climbed log ladders to the platforms where they slept at night (above).

The League of the Iroquois

Iroquois government was based on the clans. Within each longhouse lived an extended family, called the *ohwachira*, whose members were related through the female line. The oldest woman in the ohwachira, known as the clan mother, served as the leader. She supervised farming and the other group work of the women. Iroquois religious ceremonies followed the seasons and the cycles of the moon, and the clan mother was responsible for bringing people together at the appropriate time. It was she who settled disputes within the longhouse, and in consultation with other women, selected the sachem, or leader, who represented the clan in the village council. She also advised the sachem and made sure he followed the Great Law that bound the nations together in the League.

A sachem generally served for life, unless he displeased his clan mother. He was then removed or symbolically "dehorned;" that is, his traditional antler headdress was taken away from him. When a sachem died, it was the clan mother along with the other women who named a successor. All adult members of the clan voted on her choice. If approved, the new sachem assumed the name and position of his predecessor.

The village council discussed practical matters of hunting,

Not-o-way *(the Thinker), an Iroquois sachem, was painted by George Catlin. Not-o-way believed that the Iroquois had once conquered most of the world, but had lost their land when the Great Spirit inflicted a disease upon his people.*

fishing, farming, defense, religion, and ceremonies. Women did not participate directly in this council, but headed households and exercised great influence over the men. The tribe, or nation, was made up of all the villages within the territory and was represented by a council of the sachems from each of the clans. The tribal council discussed policy but lacked the authority to carry out decisions unless a consensus, or unanimous agreement, had been reached. Individual families, clans, and villages could refuse to take part in an attack on an enemy or any other action with which they disagreed.

The Roots of Peace. During the years before the formation of the League, there was constant, bloody warfare among the five tribes—the Iroquois were great warriors. French explorers had a saying: "They approach like foxes, fight like lions, and disappear like birds." Often, the Iroquois tortured their captives and occasionally they practiced cannibalism. Some captives, mostly women and children, were adopted into the tribe, usually by a family that had lost a son in battle. The others were forced to run a gauntlet in which they were beaten and jabbed by every man, woman, and child in the village, then tortured—often for days. Torture was undertaken partly to prove the courage of the captive. If he chanted his death song, without crying out, even as his fingers were chopped off and his flesh burned, the Iroquois would eat his heart so they might acquire some of his courage.

Eventually, the five tribes declared a truce among themselves and became among the best-organized of Native American nations. Their political life was centered around the League, which was established about 1570 by a prophet named Deganawida, believed to be a Huron, who visited each of the tribes and encouraged unity, and the Mohawk leader Hayenwatha, or Hiawatha, whose name means "he who seeks the wampum belt." Henry Wadsworth Longfellow mistakenly used the name for the hero of his famous poem "The Song of Hiawatha."

The Hiawatha in the poem is actually based on Manabozho, a mythical figure of the Ojibwa people. In the mid-1800s, Henry Rowe Schoolcraft, a government agent in the upper Great Lakes, began collecting Ojibwa folklore and legends, including tales about Manabozho. He also acquired stories of Hiawatha, from New York author J. V. H. Clark for his book *Notes on the Iroquois*. However, in his book, Schoolcraft confused Hiawatha with Manabozho, and Longfellow thus ascribed many legends to Hiawatha instead of Manabozho. According to legend, Manabozho dwelled in the skies but came to live with the Onondaga, the most favored tribe of the Iroquois. The real Hiawatha was a great Iroquois statesman who taught his people the art of good living— friendship, farming, and good will— and joined with Deganawida in creating the League.

According to legend, Deganawida, who is reverently referred to only as the Peacemaker by the Iroquois, traveled in a canoe of glistening white stone from his birthplace in Ontario to the warring tribes of New York. He showed how one arrow could easily

*G*eorge Catlin painted Good Hunter, a Seneca warrior, in 1831.

be broken. He then bound five arrows together and said, "If the five nations can come together and live in peace, like this bundle of arrows, then you will be very strong—so strong that this union will last forever." In the story, he also uprooted a towering white pine tree and told the men to throw their weapons into the hole. Then he replanted the Tree of Peace, with the weapons forever buried underneath it. At the top of the tree he placed an eagle to screech a warning if danger ever threatened the tree, and at its foot he extended four White Roots of Peace. "If any person or nation of people desires to live in peace," he explained, "they may find one of the Roots and follow it back to the Tree of Peace."

Although much of Hiawatha's life is now obscured by legend, about 1570 he and Deganawida, established a confederacy, or league, of the Cayugas, Mohawks, Oneidas, Onondagas, and Senecas. Since Deganawida had a speech impediment, Hiawatha preached the message of unity as he traveled among the tribes. Initially, he was strongly opposed, especially by Atotarho, a powerful Onondaga sachem.

According to legend, Atotarho had snakes growing out of his head and turtle claws for hands and feet. Despite a crippled body, he had supernatural powers—and he bitterly opposed the alliance of Iroquois nations. To gain Atotarho's support, Hiawatha had to comb the snakes out of his hair and straighten his body and spirit. Atotarho also insisted on several conditions, including that the Onondaga serve as hosts at the annual meeting of the Great Council and that they be allowed more representatives at council than any other tribe. The Onondaga were also to keep the wampum belt that was the record of the meeting and maintain the council fire that burned continually in their village. Atotarho's name became the official title of the hereditary chief.

This confederacy ended generations of warfare and became a model for the United States government. No one knows what happened to Hiawatha after the League of the Iroquois was established.

Keeping the Great Peace. The Mohawk, who were the first to accept the Great Peace and join the League, became known as the Elder Brothers. Vowing to keep peace among themselves, the five tribes founded a council of fifty sachems whose names, including Deganawida, Hiawatha, and Atotarho, have been passed down through the ages. The seat of Deganawida was always left vacant, making the number of sachems forty-nine in practice. There were nine each from the Mohawk and Oneida, fourteen from the Onondaga, ten from the Cayuga, and eight from the Seneca. Gifted men and women who had distinguished themselves also participated as a group of advisors called the Pine Tree Sachems. Although they weren't allowed to vote at council, these sachems did have the right to speak in meetings. Even if they acted contrary to the laws of the Great Peace, they could not be removed from the council, but no one would listen to their words.

These leaders met every summer in the land of the Onondaga, who came to be known as the Keepers of the Council Fire. The

Hiawatha helped the great leader Deganawida found the powerful League of the Iroquois. In this illustration of a scene from Longfellow's poem, Hiawatha woos a young woman by offering her proof of his prowess as a hunter.

Bread, as painted by George Catlin, became chief of the Oneida after his people were decimated by war, whiskey, and smallpox. Shrewd and well-educated, he worked to save his people from the onslaught of American settlers.

meeting opened with a prayer offered by the Onondaga and a thanksgiving address. These meetings lasted for several days, as sachems debated "across the fire." Because the sachems all had to agree to "speak with one voice," they often made long and eloquent speeches to persuade others in the council. As each sachem spoke, he held the strings of wampum to show that he was speaking truthfully from the heart. When the wampum was passed to another, it indicated that the truth of his words had been accepted.

The League was represented by a sacred circle and strings of wampum on the belt made with 1,800 beads or shells. The fifty strings on the wampum stood for each of the sachems. One string was slightly longer to show that the Onondaga were the Keepers of the Wampum. Wampum, which comes from the Algonquin word for "white bead," was often traded or received as a gift. The beads that glowed white indicated the harmony of being right and positive, while black or purple represented the opposite: destruction and even death. Europeans sometimes used strings or belts of wampum instead of coins, but the Iroquois never used wampum as money. Wampum belts were used to call sachems to council, and they were sent to other tribes as an invitation to join a war. Treaties between tribes and with Europeans were recorded on wampum belts. They also became a kind of writing on which Iroquois history and the meetings of the League were recorded.

Each member of the council was equal, but one chief had the authority to light the Great Council fire, or call them together. The individual members kept their power through votes and vetoes,

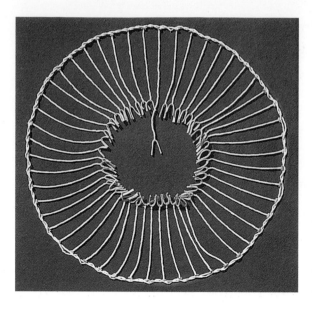

*S*trings of a circle wampum represent the League, with each string standing for one of the original chiefs.

since all leaders had to agree to a decision. The nations in the League didn't actually unite in battle against their enemies, such as the Huron, but they kept the Great Peace with each other for over three hundred years. If blood was shed within the League, instead of revenge, the victim's family was compensated with wampum or other payment of goods set by the League or tribal council. Anyone who repeatedly committed crimes, such as treason or theft, was banished from the tribe. He or she no longer had a home or family for protection.

The Iroquois viewed the League as a great longhouse, extending east to west over their land. Like a longhouse, the League contained many fires, one for each tribal family, but, like the members of a clan, they were to live together in peace. The beams of the longhouse represented each of the tribes and the rafters symbolized the laws that sheltered them. The entrances at each end were guarded—by the Mohawks, known as the Keepers of the Eastern Door, and by the Senecas, the Keepers of the Western Door.

At one time the Iroquois thought they could bring the Great Peace to all nations of the world, including the European settlers. The League of the Iroquois was a remarkable form of democratic government with a system of laws "to strengthen the house" by assuring order and prosperity among its members. Benjamin Franklin, one of the architects of the American republic, praised the League. He used it as an example of cooperation when he argued in favor of a strong union of states.

The Great Chain, or Covenant Belt, is believed to be the wampum belt presented by the United States to the Iroquois in 1794. The wampum belt represented the friendship between the thirteen states and the League of the Iroquois.

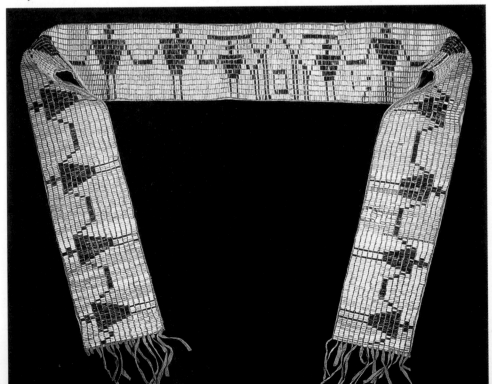

3. Lifeways

To build canoes, men made frames of ash wood, which they covered with large strips of elm bark.

*S*tanding at the center of Iroquois culture, the clan mother was the source of life in the natural world and the village, as symbolized in this painting by Richard W. Hill, a Tuscarora, in 1950.

JUST AS THE DAYS AND SEASONS FOLLOWED A CYCLE, SO TOO did the lives of the Iroquois people. Each stage of life from birth through death was marked by special practices. Midwives assisted mothers so that babies came safely into the world. Children grew up within the warm glow of their families, knowing they had a place within the clan. Adults learned to provide food, clothing, and shelter for themselves and to share with others in the village. And the dead, whether young or old, were honored in ceremonies that helped them make their way into the afterlife.

Cycle of Life

A man proved himself in battle, while a woman demonstrated courage and strength during childbirth. When a woman was about to have a baby, she moved to a special hut, along with an experienced older woman from her longhouse. The woman knelt on a deerskin and held onto a pole as the baby was born. If she cried or made any kind of noise during labor, she was scolded for not being brave.

Birth. The birth of a girl was a great blessing, because she could eventually bear more clan members and continue the cycle of generations. When a boy was born he was washed in a nearby stream or in the snow to make him strong and courageous. Babies were given a taste of animal oil to cleanse their bodies and to feed the guardian spirit that came to live in the soul from the moment of birth.

Babies received a name from the clan mother, which was

confirmed at the next village festival. Over the years, the child would receive a succession of names. All the names belonged to the clan, and none were held by two living people at the same time.

The newborn was wrapped in animal skins and strapped to a cradleboard, with sphagnum moss or cattail fluff used for a diaper. Highly decorated with clan symbols and other designs, cradleboards were about two feet long with a hood on top to shield the baby's face from sun and rain. At night babies slept with their parents or in a nearby hammock made of animal skins.

When the baby was a few days old, the mother and child returned to the shelter of the longhouse. Mothers took up their work as soon as possible, carrying their babies along with them. A piece of leather, called a burden strap, was attached to the cradleboard and wrapped around the mother's forehead, holding the baby firmly in place. Mothers often hung the cradleboards from a tree or stood them up in a corner of the longhouse. Babies could then watch their mothers work in the cornfields or at the cooking fire.

Childhood. Mothers nursed their babies for two or three years, gradually introducing a little corn soup and gruel into their diet. Living together in the longhouse family, the mother's sisters also helped in parenting, so each child had several mothers. As soon as they were strong enough, young children helped to fetch wood and water for their mothers. They carried the water in small jars.

Boys stayed close to their mothers until age eight or nine, when they began to spend time with their own group of friends. They often formed close friendships that lasted a lifetime. Girls continued to work with their mothers and the other women of the village.

Parents were very fond of their children and rarely punished them. Typically, they threw water on a misbehaving child. In serious cases, they asked a person wearing a mask of Longnose, the cannibal clown, to jump out to scare the youngster. Children were not formally educated, however, storytelling was a means of

Iroquois children learned by following the example of their parents and other adults in the village. In this re-creation, a boy watches closely as his father describes the ancient skill of making a turtle shell rattle.

Gathered at an outdoor cooking fire, blue smoke hovering around them, two children listen and watch closely as their mother and grandmother show them how to prepare corn and other staple foods.

both entertainment and instruction in the beliefs and ways of their people. During the winter months, the elders of the village told stories that included lessons about the history of their people and proper behavior.

At puberty, boys strode into the forest on a vision quest. Alone, without food, they fasted for about two weeks to induce dreams to help them discover what they would become later in life. At some point their guardian spirit revealed itself. The guardian spirit foretold the boys' future and left them with a special song. During times of danger, boys sang this song for courage and protection.

As they came of age, girls were more closely supervised by the older women of the longhouse. When they had their first menstrual period, they were considered a danger to the welfare of the village and were isolated from others. Using special pots, girls cooked and ate their food alone until they married a young man from another clan. During each menstrual period, throughout their childbearing years, women followed these same practices.

Marriage. In some Iroquois tribes, a mother suggested a possible wife for her son. If the young man liked her choice, his mother spoke to the young woman's mother, who decided if he was a skilled enough hunter and warrior to marry her daughter. The clan mother made the final decision regarding the proposed union; if she said no, the marriage could not take place. She reviewed the couple's age, suitability, and clan relations. If the marriage was approved, the young man and woman marked their courtship by an exchange of gifts, but there was no dowry. For the marriage feast, the bride made corn bread, and the groom brought meat.

The Iroquois were different from Europeans in that the bride brought her husband home with her. Even after the marriage, the woman's bonds to her clan were stronger than those to her husband. He always remained a member of his own clan and a guest in her longhouse, whereas she spent her entire life among her own clan.

Couples ideally became joined for life, and divorce was viewed unfavorably. However, if a husband proved lazy or unable to provide for his wife, she would order him to pick up his clothes, weapons, and blanket and leave the longhouse. Or she simply placed his belongings outside the doorway. Each was then free to remarry.

Death. Because of disease and war, the Iroquois did not enjoy long lives. As many as half the children died before they reached twelve years of age, and the average life span for adults was just thirty-one years.

Burial practices varied by tribe and changed over time. Early on, the Iroquois honored their dead in elaborate funerals. They placed the bodies on wooden scaffolds high above the ground, so they would be closer to the divine forces in the sky. The deceased remained on the scaffold until the body decomposed. Then the bones were bundled and buried in a kind of mass grave called an ossuary. There was usually one burial place for each village. In later times, the deceased was dressed in "dead clothes" and buried in a

*S*ilhouetted against the evening light, burial scaffolds were used to bring the dead closer to the spirits dwelling in the sky. After the body had completely decomposed, the bones were taken down, gathered in a bundle, and buried in a mass grave.

curled-up position in a bark-lined grave about three feet deep with items such as food, clothes, and weapons needed for survival in the afterlife. After contact with Europeans, the Iroquois began to bury their dead in wooden coffins.

Shortly after death, the home of the deceased was cleaned. Mirrors and other reflective objects were turned around so that no one, especially children, would be frightened by seeing the image

The Iroquois believed that the spirits of the deceased journeyed to the Land of the Dead beyond the setting sun. Supernatural forces inhabited the

of the ghost. Food was set out for the spirit of the dead person, and at least two people kept a vigil over the body.

The Iroquois believed that the spirit of the departed lingered in the village for ten days. They held the Tenth Day Feast with offerings of food, tobacco, and song to protect the living and to sustain the deceased until its spirit reached the Land of the Dead beyond the setting sun. Twice a year they held the Feast of the

heavens, and people often gazed heavenward when they prayed or made offerings to them.

Dead to help any spirits still hovering about the village on their journey along the Milky Way, the Path of the Dead. Expressing the wishes of all the mourners, a speaker chanted, "I will make the sky clear for you."

Daily Life

Iroquois society was matrilineal, meaning people traced their family tree through their mother's side of the family. Children were always considered part of their mother's clan. Should a man's wife die, he would be encouraged to marry one of her sisters, so that remarriage would not disrupt the lineage of the family. Men had little role in managing the household, which was the exclusive responsibility of the women. In fact, everything inside the longhouse belonged to the women—even the longhouse itself. Men owned only their clothes, tools, and weapons.

Women were primarily responsible for rearing the children, often putting the girls and younger boys to work in the garden. When the boys turned eight or nine, they began to spend time with other boys and with male relatives, often their uncles, to learn the roles of men among the Iroquois. Expected to be physically strong, girls helped their mothers and aunts, learning by example how to take care of the home and fields.

Girls watched their mothers make pots by rolling wet clay into a ball and then making a dent with their fists. To shape the pot, they slapped the clay with a wooden paddle as they turned the pot on their fist. Women dried the pots in the sun, then baked them in a hot fire. They didn't glaze their pots, but made patterns with fingernails, corncobs, and sticks. Girls also learned to make cornmeal by placing yellow kernels in a hollowed-out log called a mortar and pounding it with a wooden mallet called a pestle. As the givers of life, women were responsible for feeding the people of the longhouse. Since women headed households, girls were encouraged to take a leading role in their families.

Girls learned many household crafts, such as basketry and pottery, from the women of the village. Here, two girls make clay pots with their mother in the shade of a lean-to just outside the longhouse.

Corn, beans, and squash not only grew well together but could be dried and stored over the long winter. The crops were either hung from the rafters or placed in pits dug into the earth.

In early spring girls helped their mothers collect milkweed, leeks, skunk cabbage, and other tender greens to supplement their diet after the long winter. During the Berry Moon of June, at the beginning of summer, they gathered wild strawberries and celebrated the arrival of the first fruit of the year. They also picked wild plums, grapes, cherries, and crab apples along with chestnuts, black walnuts, and hickory nuts.

When the oak leaves grew to the size of a red squirrel's paw, the girls and women hilled the earth in communal fields and planted the seeds that had been soaked in water to make them sprout more readily. As a group, the women planted corn, beans, and squash—crops so interrelated and essential to Iroquois survival that they were called "the three sisters." When grown together, corn, beans, and squash kept the garden plot in balance, which was very important to all aspects of Iroquois life. Beans returned nitrogen to the soil, corn provided stalks on which the bean vines climbed, and the broad squash leaves—whether Hubbard, crookneck, or winter squash—spread over the ground to shade out weeds. Women also planted sunflowers, whose seeds could be easily stored.

Much of the autumn harvest was saved to provide food through the long winter. Women smoked or dried meat, which was stored high up in the longhouse. Corn was either hung in the longhouse or kept in a crib, a small building with open slats, that allowed air to flow around the brightly colored ears of corn.

Corn was also stored in barrels made from large, hollowed-out tree trunks. Placed inside the longhouse, the log barrels kept the precious harvest dry and protected it from hungry rodents.

Settlers later adapted similar designs for corncribs on their farms. Dried corn was also roasted to make parched corn, which stored well and provided excellent nutrition. Parched corn was placed in bark barrels and stored in pits in the ground, along with pumpkins and other kinds of squash.

Girls helped their mothers prepare meals over fires in the center aisle of the longhouse, roasting or boiling fish and wild game. They boiled water by dropping hot stones from the fire directly into clay pots. Corn was their most important source of food, and they grew several kinds including white flint, or squaw corn, and dent corn. Green ears of corn were boiled or roasted; sometimes kernels were scraped from the cob and fried in bread or used in soups. Corn

Pits dug into the ground were good, safe places to store the autumn harvest. Cool, constant temperatures preserved the food; the wooden bars kept raccoons and other hungry animals from getting inside.

soup was a favorite dish, as was succotash, a mixture of beans, corn, and hominy. To make hominy, the Iroquois boiled corn with wood ashes to loosen the hulls. Sometimes they ground the kernels of corn with a mortar and pestle and then mixed the cornmeal with maple sugar, dried berries, or chopped dried meat. People also ate corn in puddings and bread, which was often flavored with dried nuts or berries, and in soup made from strawberries and green corn. Women used gourd ladles to scoop food out of the cooking pots. People ate with wooden spoons and bowls and drank from cups made from turtle shells or carved from wood. They usually had only one meal a day, but a clay pot was always on the fire, and they could eat whenever they got hungry.

Women used mortars made from tree trunks with a bowl-shaped hollow carved into the top end. Hard kernels of corn were placed in this shallow hole and pounded into coarse yellow meal with club-shaped wooden pestles.

Corn Soup

Here is a recipe for corn soup, courtesy of Ska-Nah-Doht Iroquoian Village, which was often part of the daily meal in Iroquois longhouses. Traditionally, this recipe was made with dried white corn (large, flat kernels) that was boiled in ashes to make hominy. The hominy was then rinsed and cooked with deer meat and beans.

In this modern version, you can substitute canned hominy corn and salt pork, cooked ham, or another meat of your choice.

Ingredients:

2 19-ounce cans of hominy corn
1 pound of diced salt pork or cooked ham
1 pound of dried kidney beans

Place the hominy corn, salt pork, and kidney beans in a large pot. Add enough water to cover the ingredients and simmer for 1½ to 2 hours until the beans are tender. Add salt and pepper to taste.

Women also grew corn to provide many kinds of useful materials. Corn cakes were wrapped in corn leaves, then cooked. The juice from green stalks was applied to cuts and bruises. Dry stalks were hollowed out and plugged, then used to store medicines. Stalks were also used as toy spears and clubs. Rough cobs made good scrub brushes and stoppers for jugs, and dried yellow kernels were used as beads in rattles. Women shredded cornhusks to make filling for pillows and mattresses or wove husks into trays, baskets, mats, and slippers. Mothers made cornhusk dolls with corn silk hair for their daughters, and men fashioned ceremonial masks from the dried leaves.

In addition to farming and cooking, women crafted fine pottery and splint baskets to furnish their longhouses. They also made a versatile twine from the inner bark of elm trees. They cut the bark into narrow strips, which they boiled in ashes and water to separate into threads. Men wove the threads into fishnets, and with bone needles, women knitted the threads into lovely and useful burden straps. Women wore these straps around their heads to support cradleboards, food baskets, and wooden frames called burden carriers on their backs.

Women also made the buckskin clothing for the clan. First they tanned the deerskin—a long and difficult task that took ten to twelve days. After the deer was skinned, all the hair had to be scraped from the hide. The hide was then cleaned with a solution of hardwood ashes—which contains lye—and boiling water. The deer's brain, liver, and fat were boiled to release an oil, and the

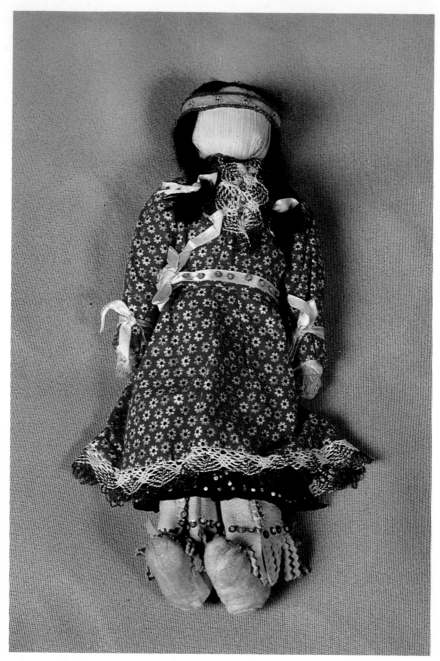

*L*oving parents, the Iroquois sometimes made toys for their children. This cornhusk doll is similar to those made by Iroquois mothers hundreds of years ago.

mixture was rubbed into the skin to soften it. The hide was then stretched on a rack and dried, after which it was smoked. Smoking toughened the buckskin and gave it a pleasing tan color.

Women gathered pieces of buckskin and sewed them together to make moccasins, breechcloths, and skirts. In warm weather, boys and men wore only a breechcloth, a piece of buckskin run between their legs and tied around their waists. Girls and women wore a knee-length skirt. During the winter, males added a jerkin, or buckskin shirt, leggings, and sometimes a kiltlike skirt. Girls and women also wore shirts and leggings as well as a longer skirt. During the winter, men and women wrapped themselves in robes of moose, buffalo, and bearskins with the fur turned inward for greater warmth.

Clothing not only offered protection but served as a form of decoration. Women often adorned finished clothing with porcupine quills and dyed moose hair. Feathers, fur, shells, bones, claws, wood, and stones such as quartz were made into jewelry and hair ornaments, many of which had religious meaning. Both men and women wore necklaces, bracelets, and earrings. During the summer, they smeared their bodies with bear grease to protect themselves from mosquitoes and blackflies. Mixing red ochre, bloodroot, and charcoal with sunflower seed oil, they also painted themselves with geometrical designs or animal figures. Men painted their faces as well—blue for health, black for war or mourning, and red for either life or violent death—and they tattooed their bodies. Women and girls braided their hair, which

1roquois women did not have cotton or wool fabrics. Instead, they relied on animal hides, especially deerskins, in making clothes for their families. The stiff hides were cured, or tanned, to make supple buckskin.

was allowed to grow long. Men usually went bareheaded. Some shaved one side of their head and let a long lock hang down from the other. Others shaved both sides of their heads, leaving a ridge of hair, called a scalp lock or roach, on top running from the hairline to the nape of their necks, which is popularly known today as a "Mohawk."

Along with the Algonquins, the Iroquois were among the first Native Americans to meet French, Dutch, and English explorers and settlers in the New World. When these Europeans began to trade with the Iroquois, wool and linen cloth replaced buckskin for clothing, because it didn't require the long tanning process and was easier to sew. From this time onward, the Iroquois generally adopted the same fashions as the settlers. Brightly colored solids and later calicos and prints were especially popular among the women, who added ribbons and woven sashes with glass beads embroidered onto the cloth in lovely floral patterns. Glass beads became the most common material for jewelry.

Hunting, Trading, and Warfare

During early summer, when elm bark was most easily stripped from the tree, men built or repaired longhouses and made canoes. Many Native Americans of the Northeast used birchbark canoes, but the Iroquois made their canoes of elm bark. They stripped large pieces of bark from the trees and removed the rough outer layer, then joined the sheets over a frame of ash wood to form a pointed canoe. An ash wood rim was run around the edge of both sides and lashed together with bark twine. The canoes ranged in length from twelve to forty feet. The biggest canoes carried up to twenty warriors and were mainly used on lakes and large rivers. Smaller canoes carried two or three people on journeys with frequent portages. Although sturdy and well-made, Iroquois canoes were thick, heavy, and slow. Whenever possible, the Iroquois stole light, fast birchbark canoes from the Algonquins.

The men cleared fields for the women in preparation for planting. The only crop grown by men was tobacco, which they smoked with sumac leaves and red willow bark. This sacred plant was believed to be a means of speaking with the spirit world, and its smoke rose to the skies during most village ceremonies. Tobacco was sprinkled on rapids to quiet the spirits living in the rivers, and small bags were attached to masks to strengthen their magic. Men also simply enjoyed a smoke in handmade clay pipes.

Men made snowshoes and household utensils and collected bones, antlers, stone, and wood to make tools. Most tool blades were shaped from a type of flint called chert. A durable stone on which a very sharp edge could be chipped, or knapped, chert was used to make points for arrows and spears, as well as blades for axes, scrapers, knives, and other tools. With stone hammers, the men knocked off bits of flint to form the general shape of the point or blade. They then used deer antlers to chip sharp edges on the blade and notches for tying the tool to a handle or the point to the shaft. Men also made tomahawks and war clubs from pieces of flint or other stones strapped to wooden handles. Hardwoods, especially hickory, maple, and cherry, were often used for weapon

$\mathbf{A}$mong the many tools, weapons, and other belongings made by Iroquois men were snowshoes. The skillfully constructed snowshoes were used to tramp over the deep drifts in winter.

Men taught their sons and nephews how to hunt. Here, a father points to a rabbit hidden in the foliage as his son takes careful aim. The small game that boys brought home was a welcome addition to the family's diet.

shafts and tool handles. Chert was also used for such items as fishnet sinkers and small hammers.

Deer and moose antlers, as well as bones, were honed into points (for arrows and spears), hair combs, musical instruments, and farming tools; the shoulder blade of the deer or a tortoise shell attached to a stick made a good hoe. Fishhooks, needles, and many other objects were fashioned from small bones, and men used sinew—the tendons in animal muscles—as a very tough string to tie arrow points to the wooden shaft. Cord was also made from strips of bark and plant stems. Tools were held tightly together with glue made from boiled fish scales and other animal parts.

In addition to repairing longhouses and making tools, the men protected their villages during times of warfare, but they were often away from home for months attacking distant tribes. In fact, most of the important tasks of the men—hunting, fighting, and trading—were undertaken away from the longhouses. The Iroquois did not have horses. Men either paddled canoes down rivers or jogged along trails, making temporary camps in the forest. Trails connected one village clearing with another and were used continually for travel and communication. A major trail that ran east to west became the backbone of the trail network—the corridor in the great "longhouse" of the League. Along this trail, the Iroquois went "from fire to fire" or "from smoke to smoke" visiting other tribes. The Iroquois also followed trails into the forest for purposes of hunting and warfare.

Boys learned to hunt and fight from their fathers and uncles (their mother's brothers), as well as how to master various crafts essential to their survival. To develop their coordination, eyesight, and aim, boys practiced their skills with bow and arrow, blowgun, and tomahawk. They learned to catch fish in nearby streams and trap small animals in the forests. To prove his courage as a hunter and warrior, a boy was left alone in the forest to defend himself against wolves and bears. He learned to "read" the land by recognizing an animal's track in the light snow.

To provide venison and other meat for their village, men hunted in the forests with bows and arrows for large game—mainly deer, black bear, elk, moose, and beaver. Deer was the primary source of meat in their diet. Bear was also prized for its greasy meat, which was used as ceremonial food, and for its thick hide, which was turned into warm blankets. Cooked beaver tail was considered a special delicacy.

Men shaped bows of sturdy hickory and strung them with a length of twisted woodchuck hide. They made arrow shafts of maple tipped with flint or bone points and feathered at the notched ends. In later years, they used blowguns to shoot rabbits, squirrels, raccoons, porcupines, and other small animals. Men also trapped bears in deadfalls and rabbits in snares. The land abounded with game birds, including ducks, geese, wild turkeys, ruffed grouse, and passenger pigeons, and hunters were skilled at bringing down feathered quarry. Fishing with spears and basket traps, as well as hooks and lines, the men provided trout, salmon, bass, perch, whitefish, and eels for their clan.

*M*en shaped points for arrows by chipping pieces of flint. The arrowheads were very sharp and effective in bringing down the white-tailed deer, elk, moose, and black bear.

Often, men hunted alone, staying out for days and living on parched corn mixed with sugar. This work required skill, patience, endurance, and a thorough knowledge of the habits of wild animals. Sometimes, a group of hunters built a V-shaped brush fence, two or three miles long on each side, and drove deer toward the narrow opening where they were shot by hunters hidden in the bushes. As many as a hundred deer could be taken in this method. In the autumn men left their longhouses for several weeks to go hunting, taking shelter in temporary camps in the forest. When the constellation Pleiades reached its highest point at dusk, they knew it was the end of the season and time to trudge back to the village on their snowshoes.

Iroquois warriors relied on three weapons: a bow, a tomahawk with a stone head, and a war club. One type of war club was made of ironwood with a thick knot on the end. Another had a deer's sharp horn attached to the end. The raid was the most common type of combat. War parties of ten to a hundred men quietly crept up to an enemy village and ambushed people as they left for the day. The warriors killed the men, taking their scalps, captured the women, and then fled homeward. Sometimes, tribes engaged in pitched battles with up to two thousand warriors on each side. They went to war to avenge a murder or other crime, to further their own prestige and personal power, to defend their lands, and to acquire captives to replace lost relatives.

Men traded with other Native American tribes, although they never had as many established trade routes as the Huron. Traveling primarily on foot, they traded with the Susquehannock, Delaware, and other tribes along the Atlantic coast as far south as present-day Florida and as far west as the Mississippi River. They exchanged food, clothing, jewelry, tools, and musical instruments for shells and other items. They in turn swapped the shells for tobacco and other goods from the Neutral and Petun Indians.

When they encountered the French and Dutch in the early 1600s, the Iroquois began to trade animal skins, especially beaver pelts, for copper kettles, cloth, glass beads, and iron axes. They also traded for forged metal tools, which were highly prized because they were easier to work with and more durable than flint tools. Men also acquired firearms early on from the Swedes, Dutch, and later the British. This enabled them to achieve great power during the colonial period of American history.

Competition in the lucrative fur trade brought the Iroquois into greater conflict with other tribes in the so-called Beaver Wars. Men also had to travel greater distances from their longhouses and were not able to hunt or work as much around the village. Their long absences made it difficult for families to provide for themselves. Traders also introduced rum, which had a devastating effect on the Iroquois. Not only did the settlers bring goods previously unknown to the Iroquois, but French Jesuits and other missionaries introduced new religions.

In addition to trading, men loved to compete among themselves in contests and games as a test of agility and endurance. Like other woodland dwellers, the Iroquois needed to be able to run fast, so boys often had races. They practiced with bows and arrows to develop their hunting skills, and they threw spears through a rolling hoop to improve their aim. Their favorite game was stickball, an early version of lacrosse. They played with a wooden stick that had a leather mitt at one end to catch and carry the ball, which was carved from wood or made of deerskin filled with hair. Games were hotly contested, even brutal, preparation for the rigors of battle, and many players were injured.

During the winter, the Iroquois played "snow snake" in which they skimmed a long, straight stick as far as possible over the snow. During the cold months, they also played games of chance and guessing games in the longhouse. One of the most popular was the Bowl Game (later called the Peach Stone Game after the introduction of the fruit). This game was played with a wooden

Played with a leather ball and rackets, stickball was the most popular Iroquois game—a test of strength and endurance—that prepared men for the rigors of hunting and warfare.

bowl and six plum seeds, or stones, painted black on one side. Each player banged the bowl on the ground, making the stones jump and land with different sides facing up. The winner was the player who had the most plum stones with either the light or dark side turned up.

Girls and women, as well as boys and men, loved sports. A favorite game was shinny, which was played with a flattened buckskin ball. Any number of players divided into two teams. Each player had a stick that resembled a field hockey stick. Goalposts were set up at each end of a field, about two hundred yards long—twice the length of a modern football field—and the object of the game was to drive the ball between the other team's goalposts.

4. Beliefs

To this day, Iroquois and other _____ _____ make dream catchers. The _____ on the _____ _____ bad dreams before they reach sleeping _____ and adults.

THE IROQUOIS BELIEVED THAT SUPERNATURAL FORCES WERE PRESENT in all things in nature. These spirit forces were created by the supreme being. Sky spirits assumed the form of wind, thunder, sun, moon, and stars. Earth spirits were found in plants and animals. All these spirit forces flowed together in *orenda*, the force that controlled the weather and all living things. Flowing like a song through nature, orenda gave people spiritual power and the ability to undertake mighty deeds.

When men and women arose in the morning they thanked the Master of Life that they were alive for another day. The Master of Life was constantly engaged in a battle with his evil brother, Flint. The Iroquois believed that a balance between good and evil was necessary for harmony in the world. People were both good and bad, just as wolves were not completely wicked, and rabbits, which nibble young green shoots of corn, were not entirely good.

The Iroquois respected the power of dreams. They devoted a great deal of time to interpreting them and loved to play a game in which they guessed each other's dreams. The dreamer offered riddles as clues or hints. For example, that which "whistles in the wind" meant the corn spirit, and an object that "has holes, yet catches" was the net on a lacrosse stick. Dreams—the wishes of the soul—were meant to be fulfilled. People believed that anything they dreamed would actually happen to them. So, if a warrior dreamed of being wounded, he would ask a friend to cut him slightly, making the dream come true in a harmless manner rather than as a serious injury in battle. Dreams and visions were also

*E*ven today, the spiritual forces of the world are recognized among Iroquois people and portrayed in their arts and crafts. These painted stones depict the clans and their relationship with the supernatural forces around them.

part of religious ceremonies. The shaman dreamed more than ordinary people and used the spirit forces that visited him in these dreams to cure illness.

The Iroquois respected the forests, the fields, and the rivers—their sources of food, clothing, and shelter. They held many rituals throughout the year before hunting and planting and said prayers of thanks that the earth had sustained them through another harvest. A hunter strove to think like the animal he stalked. By understanding the deer, he could more easily find it in the dense foliage and shadows of the woods. When he killed the animal, he knelt beside it and offered a prayer of thanks for its providing food and clothing for his family. Before he skinned the deer, he prayed that its spirit would be reborn and have a better life.

The False Face Society

The people of the longhouse believed that illness had both a physical and spiritual cause, and they formed groups called medicine societies to protect themselves. They had great faith in these societies in healing the sick and battling evil. The most famous was the False Face Society whose members wore carved wooden masks, such as "Old Broken-Nose," to frighten the spirits of disease. Members of the False Face Society performed the Traveling Rite each spring and fall to cleanse their village or to cure a person who was sick. They carved their masks out of a living tree, making offerings of tobacco smoke as they worked. They believed that if the carving was begun in the morning, the mask should be painted red; if begun in the afternoon, it should be painted black. When the mask was completed, it was cut from the tree. The group of healers came to the patient's longhouse, scraped their rattles on the walls, and screamed to scare away the evil spirits. Sometimes they were helped by another medicine society whose members wore cornhusk masks (also called "bushy head" or "fuzzy hair" masks). They danced, made tobacco offerings, and shook their rattles over the sick person.

Iroquois beliefs in healing and the spirit world are reflected in many of their stories. Here is one of their legends that over the generations was told in the flicker of orange light from the fires in the longhouses.

"The Gift of the Great Spirit"

Deep in the past, a hungry old man, covered with sores, came to a village. At the longhouse of the Turtle Clan he asked for food and shelter, but the matriarch was disgusted by the sight of him and told him to go away. Next he went to the longhouse of the Beaver Clan but was turned away again. The Wolf, Deer, Eel, Heron, and Hawk Clans also refused to help him.

Tired, the old man came to the last longhouse in the village, which belonged to the Bear Clan. Here, the clan mother welcomed him and offered him food and a bed. The next day the old man became ill, but he told the woman of a secret plant which, if prepared in a special way, would cure him.

He got better, but over the next several weeks he became sick again and again, each day with a different illness. The woman gathered herbs and prepared them as he instructed, and each time he got better. Then one day the old man changed into a handsome warrior. He told the woman that he was the Great Spirit, and because she had been kind to him he had taught her all the cures for sickness.

Since that day only the women and men who belong to the Bear Clan, which became the Keeper of the Medicine, have known the cures for many illnesses.

Ceremonies and Dances

The Iroquois held many ceremonies, which closely followed the cycle of seasons. Each moon had a name. These names described either the season or the farming, hunting, gathering, or fishing that took place under that moon: Midwinter (February), Sugar (March), Fishing (April), Planting (May), Strawberry (June), Blueberry (July), Green Corn (August), Freshness (September), Harvest (October), Hunting (November), Cold (December), Very Cold (January). During seasonal ceremonies—the Midwinter, the Planting, the Green Corn, and the Harvest—people offered thanks and danced to rekindle both old and new dreams.

Each village had a special longhouse where councils were held and ceremonial speeches, songs, and dances were offered. There was much feasting as people danced to the beat of water drums and rattles and raised their voices in song. Drums were covered with a groundhog skin and filled with water, which gave the instrument a high, clear note. Rattles were made by filling turtle shells, horns, and elm bark pouches with seeds or pebbles. The most important were the turtle rattles made with the shells of snapping, box, or mud turtles. Men also tied strings of deer hooves to leather thongs and wrapped them around their knees. Tobacco was thrown on hot coals or smoked in stone or clay pipes, its smoke rising to the heavens. Pipes were smoked to welcome an honored guest or end disputes, but they were not passed from one person to another, as among plains tribes.

In the Midwinter Ceremony, masked messengers went through the longhouses, stirring the ashes of fires gone cold, to announce the start of the ceremony. The most important festival, the Midwinter included a renewal of dreams, playing of games, and dancing. Gourd rattles called pumpkin shakes were used to keep rhythm in the dances. Dream-guessing was an important part of the celebration as well. As with all Iroquois ceremonies, the Midwinter began and ended with a prayer giving thanks. The Iroquois did not ask the supreme being for anything, but expressed gratitude for what they had already been given.

In the early spring, when they tapped maple trees for their sweet sap, people feasted, sang, and danced in the Maple Ceremony. This festival included the interpretation and acting out of dreams, the confession of sins, and the burning of tobacco. Masks and wampum were potent symbols of the spirit world. In the Thunder Ceremony, held when storms first swept across the land in the spring, the Iroquois gave thanks for the rains needed for a good crop. In gratitude for the distant thunder, they sprinkled

This rattle was made with the shell of a snapping turtle. Small pebbles were placed in the shell, which was then carefully sealed and fitted with a handle made from the turtle's head.

tobacco on the fire and enjoyed a war dance and sometimes a game of lacrosse. During the Planting Ceremony they were filled with both hope and worry. Although they did not ask for good weather for their crops, the Iroquois made offerings of shell beads and tobacco in the hope of bringing rain. If the rains did not come, they might hold another Thunder Ceremony.

In June, when wild strawberries glistened like jewels among the green foliage near the ground, the people of the longhouse held the Strawberry Ceremony in an atmosphere of good feeling. Tobacco was not necessary at this festival because strawberries grew within reach and there was no need for fragrant smoke to rise skyward to the Great Spirit. Thanksgiving was deeply felt because of the warm weather and summer abundance. A delicious strawberry drink was a special treat.

Other seasonal festivals were the Green Bean Ceremony, the Green Corn Ceremony, and the Harvest Ceremony. The Green Corn Ceremony marked the time when sweet corn had ripened and was eaten. People gave thanks that the crops had been successfully harvested. Women played a central role in this ceremony, which had to do with food for the body and the spirit.

Both the Sun and the Moon Ceremonies were usually held during a long period of clear weather. People gave thanks to these heavenly bodies. The ceremony included shooting arrows at the sun in the day and at the moon at night, and tobacco was burned so that its smoke would rise to the skies.

The most important festivals were held at the first green of early summer, the autumn harvest, and the winter solstice. The Iroquois were doing all they could to assure themselves of a good harvest and enough food to carry them through the long winter. Between these events, people entertained themselves with outdoor games during the warm months. Throughout the bitter winter, they remained in their longhouses, eating corn, nuts, and dried vegetables, along with smoked meat and fish, and listening to stories. They had great respect for anyone who could ask a clever riddle, invent a word game, or tell a good tale.

Dressed in ornate traditional regalia, this boy re-creates one of the ancient dances that have come down as part of the many seasonal ceremonies in which prayers are offered for an abundant harvest or a good hunt.

5. Changing World

By the late 1700s, most Iroquois families had abandoned their longhouses in favor of hand-hewn log cabins. They also adopted Western-style dress and made use of many new tools and goods.

IN THE MID-1600S THE LEAGUE BECAME VERY POWERFUL WHEN the Iroquois crushed the Hurons and then defeated the other tribes around them. The French had been trying unsuccessfully to conquer the Iroquois since the explorer Samuel de Champlain had routed a Mohawk war party in 1609. By the middle of the 1700s, however, the Iroquois dominated all of New York and lower Canada—from the St. Lawrence River to the shores of Lake Erie.

From the time Europeans first arrived in North America, the world of the Iroquois had begun to change. Originally, the Iroquois viewed these new people as trading partners. Because of their powerful, well-established confederacy, they did not feel threatened by the Europeans. However, the pressure of war between the foreign powers eventually caused the tribes of the League to break their neutrality and to play a powerful role as the French and the English struggled for control of North America, especially around the Canadian border. Except for the Mohawk and Cayuga, who fell under the influence of Jesuit missionaries, the Iroquois sided with the British and were largely responsible for protecting the western flank of the English colonies from the French. The League played a pivotal role in the British victory over the French in the French and Indian Wars, and after defeating the Illinois, Ojibwa, and other Great Lakes tribes, their power extended all the way to the Mississippi River. Yet many warriors were killed in these fierce battles. Smallpox and other diseases also reduced the Iroquois population, and settlers took more and more land.

With the arrival of European explorers, missionaries, and settlers, the world of the Iroquois changed forever. This engraving depicts an Onondaga village under attack by French soldiers and their allies in 1615.

During the American Revolution, the League decided to remain neutral, but eventually the Tuscarora and Oneida supported "the thirteen fires," as they called the colonies, while the other tribes maintained "the bright chain of friendship" with the British. Warriors raided the American frontier to induce settlers to abandon their farms so that the revolutionary army would be denied provisions. The League was thus split by a war that did not directly involve the member tribes, yet which cost them many lives. An old warrior recalled, "If all the skulls of the Oneida Indians killed by British forces in fighting to help the colonials get their freedom were piled together, the pile would be larger than the state capital in Albany." Thayendanegea, a Mohawk warrior also known as Joseph Brant, became a colonel in the British army and led troops into battle in the Revolutionary War. After the British lost the war, Brant led his people to safety in southern Ontario. They settled at Grand River, near the town of Brantford, named after their leader. The Cayuga also moved to Canada, where they and the Mohawk still live in the province of Ontario.

The tribes that remained in America faced many hardships. In 1779, an American general named John Sullivan attacked the Iroquois, burning their villages and fields. Afterward the Iroquois began to decline in power. After the war, the Tuscarora were scattered, although a few found a home among the Mohawk. Many of the Oneida moved to Wisconsin, while the Seneca and

Thayendanegea, or Joseph Brant, was a British supporter during the American Revolution. After the war, Brant fled to Canada and secured land for his followers at present-day Brantford, Ontario.

Onondaga remained in western New York. Red Jacket, the great Seneca leader, stated, "Your forefathers crossed the great water and landed on this island. Their numbers were small. We took pity on them, and they sat down among us. We gave them corn and meat. They gave us poison in return."

Mohawk Language

Each of the Iroquois tribes spoke its own language, although each of the tongues is similar enough to be understood by members of the other tribes. Onondaga was spoken at council, which has given this language great prominence among the Iroquois. Yet Mohawk is one of the languages that is still widely spoken today.

There are a number of ways in which Native American languages may be presented in written English. Two of the more popular books describing the Mohawk language are *One Thousand Useful Mohawk Words* and *Mohawk Language Dictionary*. The following examples are based upon the latter.

The Mohawk language has six vowels pronounced as follows:

a as in f*a*ther

e as in th*ey*, and sometimes as in m*e*t

i as in s*ee* and sometimes as in h*i*t

o as in n*o*te

en as in the nasalized "u" of s*u*n

on as in the nasalized "oo" sound in s*oo*n

The Mohawk language consists of eight consonants:

t as in *dog* or as *t*ake between consonants and at the end of a word

k as in *g*eese when before a vowel and as *k*ite other times

s as in *s*un, and as in *sh*out when followed by "i" and another vowel

r as in a combined English "r" and "l." The Mohawk "r" is difficult to pronounce. In some languages, the letter sounds more like an "l."

h as in *h*at, with an aspiration, or puff of air, for emphasis

: This is a glottal stop or pause that doesn't exist in English. It's similar to the "t" in the English "about three," when spoken rapidly.

Some consonants may be combined as follows:

kh as in *k*ite

kw as in *q*uiet, except when preceded by a consonant where the "k" takes on more of a "g" sound

th as in *th*ere, but with greater emphasis on the "h"

ts as in a combined English "j" and "ch" sound that often occurs before the "i" sound

wh as in *f*ather

Accented vowels and syllables are written in capital letters. Here are some examples of everyday words that you might say in the Mohawk language.

boy	akSA:a
brothers	rontate:KENwha:
cat	takos
child	ekSA:a
corn	Onenhste
cradleboard	karhon:
cricket	taraktarak
deer	ohskenONton
dog	rhar
earth	onhwentsia:
father	rake:NIha:
fish	kentsion:
forest	karha:
friend	onkiaTENron
frog	tskwahrhe:
girl	ekSA:a
home	ki:teRONtaks
house	kanonhsa:
maple	watha:
maple syrup	ohNEkari
mother	ihsta
mountain	onONta:
no	iah

path	ohaha:
sister	khe:kEN:a
squirrel	aROsen
sun	karahkwa:
water	ohNEka:
yes	HEN:ENhen

6. New Ways

At the turn of the century, Iroquois people
struggled to preserve traditional ways in a
modern world. In this 1910 photograph, these
people present in Iroquois headdresses with
examples of artwork — a basket and strings of
wampum.

AROUND 1800, A SENECA RELIGIOUS LEADER NAMED HANDSOME LAKE saw his people lose most of their land. Forced onto small reservations, they found it difficult to adjust to confinement and the destruction of their culture. Men, in particular, no longer ruled the world beyond the edge of the forest. Confined to farming and village affairs on the reservation, they were no longer allowed to hunt, fight, or trade beyond the village clearing. Many slid into alcoholism, and the reservations became pockets of poverty in the wilderness. In 1799, Handsome Lake, himself sick and alcoholic, appeared to fall dead. However, he had only lapsed into a coma during which he had a series of visions. Upon awakening, he declared that he had been taken on a spiritual journey by four messengers. He quit drinking and regained his health. Then the sixty-four-year-old man began speaking to his people about *Gai'wiio*, or the Good Message as he called his new religion, which was a blend of Quaker and traditional Iroquois beliefs. He opposed many white customs, especially the consumption of alcohol, and advocated purification through traditional beliefs. He urged followers to strengthen family and community bonds, share among themselves, and take up farming as a way of life. Handsome Lake helped his followers adapt to a new world. Many Iroquois who call themselves "the Longhouse People" still follow his teachings and repeat his speeches from memory.

North America has changed dramatically since the first European settlers arrived on the Atlantic coast in the 1600s. Vast areas of wilderness have vanished, and cities and towns have

By the nineteenth century, many Iroquois took up farming. Others practiced traditional skills, such as basketmaking. Here, a group of St. Regis Mohawks photographed in 1894 display their handmade wares.

sprung up across the continent. Like other Native Americans, the Iroquois were driven from their homelands or restricted to small remnants of their ancient lands. Today, many Iroquois people live in urban areas as well as on reservations.

Yet each of the tribes of the League is experiencing a rekindling of its culture, its roots extending from deep in the past to the bustle of modern life. Some ceremonies and beliefs have persisted into the late twentieth century despite hundreds of years of pressure to embrace a Western way of life. Moreover, individuals have become teachers, doctors, engineers, and other professionals. Of special renown are the Mohawk steelworkers who have been working on girders, high in the sky, constructing bridges and skyscrapers for over a hundred years. In 1883, a group of Mohawks from the St. Regis Reservation found work constructing a bridge at Cornwall, Ontario, in Canada. Other Mohawks worked on bridges spanning the St. Lawrence River. Men continue to be drawn to this dangerous work, which requires the keen sight, courage, and agility prized by their ancestors. It is believed that they also excel at this work because of their remarkable sense of balance when walking the narrow ribbons of steel. High steel allows men to work in ways similar to their forefathers—away from home for long periods of time, providing a good livelihood for their families. The risky work also offers a prestige similar to that of ancient chiefs.

At mid-century, the populations of reservations had recovered from the lows of 1900, and many families were enjoying some prosperity. Despite state and national policies, the Iroquois have refused to become simply another American minority, though leaders still worry that their heritage will be lost. The greatest threat since World War II has been federal attempts to eliminate reservations, especially the homes of the Oneida of Wisconsin and the Seneca-Cayuga of Oklahoma. Today, over 50,000 Iroquois live in the United States and Canada—more than at the height of power for the League. Many live on reservations in New York, although there are three reserves in Canada and also reservations in Wisconsin and Oklahoma.

The longhouses, stone tools, canoes, and buckskin clothes have faded into the past, but many beliefs and customs have endured among the people of the longhouse. At least one longhouse stands in each Iroquois region, no longer as a dwelling, but as a center for religious, political, and social activities. The Iroquois have a proud history, which began long before the arrival of the first Europeans, and a culture that flourishes to this day.

The cycle of ceremonies is followed by many people, and the councils continue to meet and make decisions for the Six Nations, according to the Great Law of Peace. The Great Council still meets, and clan mothers appoint sachems, although modern tribal chiefs are now elected. Members of the False Face Society still dance in masks to insure good health for their people. Artists honor the past through the practice of traditional crafts, and the language of each of the Six Nations is still spoken. Clan mothers still name the children of the clan, and on long winter nights, old men tell stories of the past to the children gathered around them.

Working on the steel girders of tall buildings and bridges, Mohawk "skywalkers" demonstrate courage and skill, as illustrated in this 1983 painting by Arnold Jacobs, an Onondaga.

A. JACOBS '83

More About

the Iroquois

Time Line

1535 French explorer Jacques Cartier sails up the St. Lawrence River and through Iroquois country

1570–1600 Hiawatha and Deganawida found the League of the Iroquois

1609 The Dutch discover the Iroquois Nation

1609–1615 Samuel de Champlain, the governor of New France, helps enemies of the Iroquois attack the Mohawk people

1640s The Iroquois begin the so-called Beaver Wars against the tribes of the upper Great Lakes

1662 A smallpox epidemic sweeps through the Iroquois, decimating their population

1666 The French begin a series of attacks on the Mohawks

1667 The five tribes of the League agree to a border treaty with the French and their Native American allies

1672 The Iroquois negotiate a peace treaty with the Algonquins regarding northeastern borders

1687 The Iroquois conquer the Illinois, Miami, Ottawa, and Hurons

1689–1763 The Iroquois take part in a series of wars between the English and French, including King William's War (1688–1697), Queen Anne's War (1702–1713), King George's War (1744–1748), and the French and Indian War (1754–1763), collectively known in North America as the French and Indian Wars

early 1700s The Iroquois Nation attains the peak of its military strength

1709 The Iroquois break neutrality in Queen Anne's War and aid England

1713 Queen Anne's War comes to an end

about 1722 The Tuscarora join as nonvoting members of the League of the Iroquois

1779 American soldiers attack Iroquois villages during the Revolutionary War

1784 The Iroquois give up most of their land to the United States in the Treaty of Fort Stanwix

1800 Seneca leader Handsome Lake establishes the Good Message religion which is still widely practiced today

1823 The Oneida begin moving to land near Green Bay, Wisconsin

1838 The Ogden Land Company takes Seneca land at Buffalo Creek

1887 The Dawes General Allotment Act encourages assimilation of native peoples into American society and calls for allotment of reservation lands to individuals

1900 Populations on reservations drop to the lowest numbers ever and tribal leaders fear that traditional culture will become extinct

1927 Clinton Rickard, a Tuscarora, organizes the Indian Defense League of America

1950s Despite Seneca protests, the United States Army Corps of Engineers builds a dam on the Cornplanter Reservation

1966 Robert L. Bennett, an Oneida, becomes head of the Bureau of Indian Affairs

Notable People

Louis Deerfoot Bennett (1830–1896), also known as Hottsasodono, meaning "he peeks in the door," was born on the Cattaraugus Reservation near Buffalo, New York. As a young man, he was given the name Deerfoot when he outran a horse. After establishing a reputation as a runner in the United States, he traveled to England in search of more track meets and greater prize money. In the early 1860s, he won many long-distance races, usually between four and twelve miles. With his substantial earnings, he returned to the United States in 1863 and organized a traveling group of runners who entertained audiences around the country. Retiring in 1870, he returned to his home on the Cattaraugus Reservation.

Black Kettle (died 1697) was an Onondaga chief who, as a supporter of the British cause, led his warriors in many battles against the French and their Native American allies. He and his band of warriors raided many settlements and trading posts west of Montreal and also headed attacks on the Algonquins as they attempted to trade with the French. In July 1692, Black Kettle led a group of warriors in an assault on Montreal, escaping with many prisoners. Five years later, he negotiated a peace treaty with the French, but before it was finalized, he was killed by an Algonquin during a hunting trip in what is now western New York.

Black Kettle

Beth Brant (1941–), a Mohawk from Ontario, Canada, is a well-known poet, storyteller, editor, and lecturer. She edited *A Gathering of Spirit* (1989), a highly regarded collection of writing and art by Native American women. She has been a lecturer at the University of British Columbia and has made many public appearances. Her work has been included in numerous anthologies and journals. Her own books include *Mohawk Trail* (1985) and *Food & Spirits* (1991). Dividing her time between homes in Michigan and Canada,

Brant is currently working on a book of essays about land and spirit.

Joseph Brant (1742–1807), whose Indian name Thayendanegea means "he places two bets," was a great Mohawk leader. As a young warrior, he saw considerable action in the French and Indian Wars as a British ally. During the American Revolution, he again sided with the British and became a colonel in the British army, fighting alongside General Burgoyne's soldiers. After the war, many Mohawks fled to Canada and Brant persuaded the king of England to give the Iroquois a land tract in what is now the province of Ontario. Known as Brant County, it is still home to many Mohawk Indians and other Iroquois descendants.

Molly Brant (about 1735–1796), the sister of Joseph Brant, married William Johnson, an officer in the British army in a Mohawk ceremony in 1753. When Johnson was knighted for his victory at Lake George in 1755, Molly came to be called Lady Johnson. Serving as hostess at Johnson Hall, she and her husband had eight children.

After her husband's death in 1774, Lady Johnson provided intelligence on American troop movements in the Mohawk valley during the American Revolution. Throughout the war, she continued to be influential among the Iroquois. After the war, she settled in Ontario and was awarded a yearly pension from the British government.

Cornplanter (about 1735–1836) was the son of a white trader and a Senaca mother. After his father abandoned him, Cornplanter grew up to become a chief during the French and Indian Wars, taking part in raids against the British. However, during the American Revolution, he formed an alliance with the British. After the war, he negotiated and signed several treaties with the Americans and often protested the mistreatment of Native Americans. Cornplanter encouraged the adoption of white ways, especially farming practices. In 1796, he received a tract of land in Pennsylvania as

Cornplanter

a reward for his services. Half brother of Handsome Lake, he received a vision late in life guiding him to end all relations with whites and he subsequently destroyed all the gifts he had received from officials over the years. In 1960, despite a bitter protest from the Senecas, the Army Corps of Engineers built Kinzua Dam, flooding 10,500 acres, including Cornplanter's land and his grave.

Hancock (active early 1700s), also known as King Hancock, was a leader in the Tuscarora War of 1711–1713. Originally, the Tuscaroras were friendly toward settlers on their homeland in present-day North Carolina— despite abuses by whites. When Swiss colonists drove Tuscarora families off their land without payment, warriors responded with a series of bloody raids. The Carolina colonies sent in troops, many of them Yamasee Indians, to attack Hancock's principal village of Cotechney. The violence continued until 1713 when Tuscarora survivors escaped northward and settled among the five nations of the Iroquois League. Around 1722, the Tuscaroras formally became the sixth nation in the confederacy.

Handsome Lake (about 1735–1815), half brother of Cornplanter and uncle of Red Jacket, grew up in a traditional Seneca family near present-day Avon, New York. Founder of a new Iroquois religion, he encouraged his people to abandon warfare and learn to farm with horses and plows. Like traditional Iroquois, he received his messages and power from dreams and visions. Handsome Lake was elected to the tribal council in 1801, and he became one of the Seneca leaders to meet with President Thomas Jefferson in Washington, D. C. He strongly opposed the loss of Native American lands and the sale of alcohol to his people. In 1850, his beliefs were outlined in the Code of Handsome Lake. As practiced today by followers who still gather in a longhouse, the Longhouse, or Good Message, religion is a blend of Quakerism and Iroquois beliefs. The religion emphasizes good deeds and silent prayer.

Hendrick (about 1680–1755) was Mahican by birth, but raised by the Mohawks. In 1710, he was one of four Native Americans, touted as "the four kings of the New World," to visit Queen Anne's court in London. When he returned to New York, Hendrick became a spokesperson for the

League. A British ally and Protestant convert, he opposed the French but also criticized British failure to defend the frontier. At the battle of Lake George in 1755, he led a band of Mohawk warriors along with British troops under the leadership of William Johnson against the French and their Native American allies. Johnson received knighthood for this great victory, but Hendrick and many of his warriors lost their lives in this battle.

Emily Pauline Johnson (1862–1913), the daughter of a Mohawk chief and an English mother, attended Indian schools through the elementary level. An avid reader, by age twelve, she had read many of the literary classics and, as a teenager, she began to have her poems published in literary journals. Her first reading in Toronto in 1892 received high praise and for the next eighteen years she made many public appearances in the United States, Canada, and England. Dressed as an Indian princess, she read her poems and celebrated both her Mohawk and Canadian heritage. Her collections of poetry, including *White Wampum* (1895), *Canadian Born* (1903), and *Flint and Feather* (1913), were very well-received. She published a collection of tales, *Legends of Vancouver* (1911), and a novel, *The Shagganappi* (1913).

Oren R. Lyons (1930–) is a professor of American Studies at the State University of New York, Buffalo. A chief of the Turtle Clan of the Onondaga Nation, he is a fine artist and publisher of *Daybreak*, a national Indian news magazine. He has also represented the interests of Native American peoples in the United Nations. "The West didn't get wild until the white people got there," he once said. "There's no such word as 'wild' in the Indian languages. The closest we can get to it is the word 'free'."

Oren R. Lyons

Ely Parker (about 1828–1895) studied law but was not allowed to be a lawyer because as an Indian he was not considered a citizen.

Ely Parker

Grandson of Red Jacket, he collaborated with Lewis Henry Morgan on the book *League of the Hodenosaunee or Iroquois* published in 1851. A year later, Parker became chief of the Seneca and helped the Tonawanda Seneca keep their reservation. During the Civil War, he served on the staff of General Ulysses S. Grant and wrote down the terms of Robert E. Lee's surrender at Appomattox. When Grant became president he appointed Parker to be the first Native American to become commissioner of Indian affairs. In this position, Parker worked to maintain peace with Red Cloud and the Oglala Sioux. "If any tribe remonstrated against the violation of their natural and treaty rights, members of the tribe were shot down and the whole treated as mere dogs," he said. "Retaliation generally followed, and bloody Indian wars have been the consequence, costing lives and much treasure." Fed up with corruption in the United States government, Parker resigned in 1871.

Maris Bryant Pierce (1811–1874), who was also known as Hadyanodoh, or Swift Runner, was a Seneca activist who battled greedy speculators who wanted to trick Native Americans into selling their land at very low prices. While still a student at Dartmouth College he came to oppose the Treaty of Buffalo Creek of 1838, which called for the sale of Seneca land to the Ogden Land Company and removal of the tribe to Indian Territory in present-day Oklahoma. The tribe lost some of its land, including the Buffalo Creek reservation but was able to retain other reservations because of Pierce's many efforts. In later years, he became an interpreter for the Seneca Nation and helped the tribe adopt an elective system of government. Pierce once stated, "The fact that the whites want our land imposes no obligation on us to sell it, nor does it hold forth an inducement to do so, unless it leads them to offer a price equal in value to us."

Red Jacket (about 1758–1830) was an outstanding orator and a great Seneca leader. At the start of the American Revolution he advocated neutrality but joined the Mohawks, Onondagas, Cayugas, and other Senecas in support of the British. He was named because of the red coat he wore while serving as a dispatch carrier. After the war, he became the principal spokesperson for the Senecas and sometimes the entire League. An advocate of traditional customs, he opposed the efforts of missionaries to convert his people to Christianity. Shortly before his death, he said, "I am an aged tree and can stand no longer. My leaves are fallen, my branches are withered, and I am shaken by every breeze. Soon my aged trunk will fall."

Kateri Tekakwitha (1656–1680) was the daughter of a Mohawk chief and an Algonquin captive. When she was only four years old, her parents and baby brother died in a smallpox epidemic. Kateri was left badly scarred but survived the disease. Growing up in a Mohawk village in New York, she became known for her skill and hard work in making wampum.

When she was twenty years old, she was baptized and practiced Catholicism despite persecution from her own people. In 1677, she fled to Canada with a group of Christianized Oneidas. A devout Christian, she hoped to establish a convent, but church authorities rejected her plan. When she died, it is said that a miracle took place—her pockmarks disappeared. In 1884, Kateri became a candidate for canonization. In 1943, she was declared venerable and in 1980, she was declared blessed, which is the second step toward becoming a saint.

Kateri Tekakwitha

Glossary

breechcloth A cloth or skin worn between the legs; also breechclout

burden carrier A wooden frame strapped to the back for carrying goods

clan A number of families related to a common ancestor

clan mother A respected elder of the longhouse who provided leadership

False Face Society A group of men who wore carved wooden masks, such as "Old Broken-Nose," to frighten the spirits of disease

Good Message Religion established by Handsome Lake in 1799, now called the New Religion

Hodenosaunee Iroquoian name for themselves, meaning "people of the longhouse"

Irinakhoiw Ojibwa name for the Iroquois, meaning "poisonous snakes"

Iroquoian language A large language group comprising many languages spoken by Native Americans

Iroquois General names for the six nations (Mohawk, Oneida, Onondaga, Cayuga, Seneca, and Tuscarora); pronounced EAR-ah-koy in the United States and EAR-ah-kwah in Canada

Iroquois Confederacy The political union of the six Iroquois nations also referred to as the League of the Iroquois

longhouse A large dwelling covered with elm bark in which several Iroquois families lived

ohwachira An extended family, including a mother's sisters, brothers, and children, who lived together in a longhouse

orenda A supernatural force present in all things in nature

SkaNahDoht Iroquoian word meaning "a village stands again"

Sky World Iroquoian term for the place above the earth where life originated

succotash A mixture of corn, beans, and hominy that was a staple in the diet of tribes of eastern North America

three sisters Iroquoian name for corn, squash, and beans, the three primary and interrelated crops

Turtle Island The earth (formed on the back of a turtle, according to the Iroquois story of creation); figuratively North America

wampum beads made of white or purple shells; formerly psewn into belts in patterns that symbolized the history of the Iroquois people

Further Information
Readings

Over the years many fine books have been written about the six tribes that make up the Iroquois people. Among them, the following titles were very helpful in researching and writing *The Iroquois*:

Beauchamp, William M. *Iroquois Folk Lore: Gathered from the Six Nations of New York*. Port Washington, NY: Ira J. Friedman, 1922.

Encyclopedia of North American Indians. Tarrytown, NY: Marshall Cavendish, 1997.

Hirschfelder, Arlene, and Kreipe de Montaño, Martha. *The Native American Almanac: A Portrait of Native America Today*. New York: Prentice Hall, 1993.

Johansen, Bruce E., and Grinde, Donald A. Jr. *The Encyclopedia of Native American Biography: Six Hundred Life Stories of Important People from Powhatan to Wilma Mankiller*. New York: Henry Holt, 1997.

Johnson, Michael G. *The Native Tribes of North America: A Concise Encyclopedia*. New York: Macmillan, 1994.

Kimm, S. C. *The Iroquois: A History of the Six Nations of New York*. Middleburgh, NY: Press of Pierre W. Danforth, 1900.

Langer, Howard J., ed. *American Indian Quotations*. Westport, CT: Greenwood Press, 1996.

Lyford, Carrie A. *Iroquois: Their Art and Crafts*. Blaine, WA: Hancock House Publishers Ltd., 1989.

Lyford, Carrie A. *Iroquois Crafts*. Stevens Point, WI: R. Schneider Publishers, 1982.

Onondaga County Parks. Office of Museums and Historical Sites. *Sainte Marie Among the Iroquois: Educational Resource Packet*. Liverpool, NY: Onondaga County Parks, 1996.

Parker, Arthur C. *Seneca Myths and Legends*. Lincoln, NE: University of Nebraska Press, 1989.

Shanks, Ralph, and Shanks, Lisa Woo. *The North American Indian Travel Guide*. Petaluma, CA: Costano Books, 1993.

Snow, Dean R. *The Iroquois*. Cambridge, MA: Blackwell Publishers, 1994.

Speck, Frank Gouldsmith. *The Iroquois: A Study in Cultural Evolution.* Bloomfield Hills, MI: Cranbrook Institute of Science, 1945.

Spittal, William Guy, ed. *Iroquois Women: An Anthology.* Ohsweken, Ont.: Irocrafts, 1990.

Waldman, Carl. *Encyclopedia of Native American Tribes.* New York: Facts on File, 1988.

——*Who was who in Native American History: Indians and NonIndians from Early Contacts Through 1900.* New York: Facts on File, 1990.

Young people who wish to learn more about the Iroquois will enjoy these excellent books for children which were also consulted in preparing *The Iroquois:*

Doherty, Craig A., and Doherty, Katherine M. *The Iroquois.* New York: Franklin Watts, 1989.

Graymont, Barbara. *The Iroquois.* New York: Chelsea House, 1988.

McCall, Barbara A. *The Iroquois.* Vero Beach, FL: Rourke Publications, 1989.

Maracle, David Kanatawakhon. *One Thousand Useful Mohawk Words.* Guilford, CT: AudioForum, 1992.

Ridington, Jillian, and Ridington, Robin. *People of the Long House: How the Iroquoian Tribes Lived.* Vancouver: Douglas & McIntyre, 1982.

Sherrow, Victoria. *The Iroquois Indians.* New York: Chelsea House, 1992.

Sneve, Virginia Driving Hawk. *The Iroquois: A First Americans Book.* New York: Holiday House, 1995.

Wolfson, Evelyn. *The Iroquois: People of the Northeast.* Brookfield, CT: Millbrook Press, 1992.

There are over eighty versions of the Creation Story. The story appearing in this book was adapted from several other tellings and a portion of the story told at SkaNahDoht Iroquoian Village. Similarly, "The Gift of the Great Spirit" is adapted from a story told at SkaNahDoht and an account by Erminnie A. Smith published in "Myths of the Iroquois" *Second Annual Report of the Bureau of Ethnology, 1880–1881.*

Websites

Over the past few years, American Indians have made themselves known on the Internet. Here are some of the best and most interesting websites to visit for more information about the six tribes of the Iroquois and other native peoples.

American Indians Link Exchange
http://www.cris.com/~misterg/award/whoshot.shtml
First Nations: Histories
http://www.dickshovel.com/Compacts.html
FirstNations.Com
http://www.firstnations.com
HAUDENOSAUNEE (Mohawk Nation Council of Chiefs)
http://www.slic.com/~mohawkna
Iroquois
http://www.nativeauthors.com/search/tribe/iroquois.html
Iroquois History
http://www.dickshovel.com/iro.html
The Mohawk Nation of Akwesasne
http://www.cyberpoint.co.uk/mohawk/index.htm
Native American Navigator
http://www.ilt.columbia.edu/k12/naha/nanav.html
Native American Sites
http://www.pitt.edu/~lmitten/indians.html
NativeWeb
http://www.nativeweb.org/
Oneida Indian Nation
http://oneweb.org/oneida/
The Seneca Nation of Indians
http://www.localnet.com/~sni/
The Six Nations of the Iroquois
http://www.syracuse.com/discover/guide/iroquois.html
Tuscarora and Six Nations Indian Owned Websites
http://www.tuscaroras.com/

Organizations

Cayuga Nation
P. O. Box 11
Versailles, NY 14168
(716)532-4847

Oka Indian Reserve (Mohawk)
113 Rue St. Jean Baptiste
Oka, Quebec JON 1EO Canada
(514)479-8530

Oneida Nation of New York
P. O. Box 1, West Road
Oneida, NY 13421
(315)697-8251

Oneida Tribe of Indians of Wisconsin
P. O. Box 365
Oneida, WI 54155-0365

Onondaga Nation
P. O. Box 319B
Nedrow, NY 13120
(315)469-8507

St. Marie Among the Iroquois
P. O. Box 146
Liverpool, NY 13088
(315)453-6767

St. Regis Mohawk Tribe
Community Building
Hogansburg, NY 13655
(518)358-2272

Seneca Iroquois National Museum
Broad Street Extension
Salamanca, NY 14779
(716)945-1738

Seneca Nation
P. O. Box 231
Salamanca, NY 14081
(716)945-1790

SenecaCayuga InterTribal Council
Hwy 144
Miami, OK
(918)542-4486

Six Nations Indian Preserve
Ohsweken Post Office
Ohsweken, Ontario N0A 1M0
(519)445-4528

SkaNahDoht Iroquoian Village
Lower Thames Valley Conservation Authority
R. R. 1
Mount Brydges, Ontario NOL 1WO
(519)264-2457

The Six Nations

Today the Iroquois are scattered throughout upstate New York, Wisconsin, and Ontario, Canada. Here is a summary of the current status of each of the Six Nations.

The Onondaga Nation

Occupying 7,300 acres, the Onondaga Nation is located about five miles south of Syracuse, New York. Around 1,475 people are enrolled, or officially registered, members of the tribe on the reservation. Like their ancestors, the Onondaga still call themselves Hodenosaunee, the "people of the longhouse."

The nation is led by a tribal government of fourteen chiefs and one head chief, selected by the clan mothers. As Keepers of the Council Fire, the Onondaga still host meetings of the Great Council of all Six Nations on the reservation.

The Oneida Nation

Many Oneidas live on a reservation near Green Bay, Wisconsin. About 40 of the 630 people of the Oneida Nation live on a small reservation located south of the city of Oneida, New York—the smallest reservation among the Six Nations. Their thirty-two acres are all that remain of the six million acres in New York State that belonged to their ancestors. This traditionalist group was finally recognized by the Bureau of Indian Affairs in 1987, after which a longhouse was built in Oneida territory—the first in over 150 years.

Known as the People of the Standing Stone, the Oneidas acquired their name from the legend that whenever they moved, a stone appeared and gave directions. Until the Oneidas are united, it is said, the stone will no longer guide them.

The Seneca Nation

The Seneca Nation now has about 5,400 members living in the Allegheny River valley in upstate New York. The Senecas, who once inhabited half the state, now live on just over 52,000 acres spread over three reservations: the Allegany, the Cattaraugus, and Oil Springs Reservations.

The Seneca are Keepers of the Western Door, the only Iroquois tribe to own a city—Salamanca, New York, which is located on land leased to its residents from the Allegany Indian Reservation. There are three other Seneca settlements in the United States and Canada: the Tonawandas live on 7,549 acres near Akron, Ohio; another group lives on the Six Nation, or Grand River, Reserve near Brantford, Ontario; and the Seneca-Cayugas, who were relocated to northeastern Oklahoma, still live there on a 5,000-acre reservation.

The Tuscarora Nation

Today, about one thousand Tuscaroras live on their own reservation in Niagara County, north of Buffalo, New York. After battling against colonial settlers, the Tuscaroras fled north from North Carolina in the 1700s to become the sixth nation of the confederacy. In the early part of the eighteenth century, they lived in six towns protected by twelve hundred warriors.

Most of the land claims of the Tuscaroras are now being made in North Carolina where they hope to recover a portion of their former homeland.

The Mohawk Nation

The St. Regis Mohawk Reservation occupies 14,640 acres spanning the United States–Canadian border along the St. Lawrence River. Involved with the two countries and three tribal governments of their own, the 8,000 Mohawks living on the reservation experience one of the most complicated situations of any of the tribes in the Northeast. There is a council on the Canadian side of the reservation, another on the American, and a Tribal Council that oversees all activities. The reservation is confronting great economic difficulty—an aging population, substandard housing, and an unemployment rate approaching fifty percent.

The Cayuga Nation

Today, tribal enrollment for the Cayuga Nation is small—only about 1,000 people. The Cayuga do not have a reservation or own any land as a group. Most members live on or near the Seneca Nation reservation in New York or on reserves of other tribes in Canada.

Index

Page numbers for illustrations are in **boldface**.

Raymond Bial

HAS PUBLISHED OVER THIRTY CRITICALLY ACCLAIMED BOOKS OF PHOTOGRAPHS for children and adults. His photo-essays for children include *Corn Belt Harvest*, *Amish Home*, *Frontier Home*, *Shaker Home*, *The Underground Railroad*, *Portrait of a Farm Family*, *With Needle and Thread: A Book About Quilts*, *Mist Over the Mountains: Appalachia and Its People*, *Cajun Home*, and *Where Lincoln Walked*.

He is currently immersed in writing *Lifeways*, a series of books about Native Americans. As with his other work, Bial's deep feeling for his subjects is evident in both the text and illustrations. He travels to tribal cultural centers, photographing homes, artifacts, and surroundings and learning firsthand about the national lifeways of each of these peoples.

A full-time library director at a small college in Champaign, Illinois, he lives with his wife and three children in nearby Urbana.